M000086033

World of
SPORTS

Ben Groundwater
Illustrations by Paul Reid

Hardie Grant

TRAVEL

Contents

Introduction iv

•

Event calendar 1

North America 9

Brutality on ice: ice hockey 10

Friday night lights: American football 12

Holding court: basketball 13

The Friendly Confines: baseball 14

Brush with greatness: curling 16

Masked crusaders: lucha libre 18

Skate or die: skateboarding 20

Cold as ice: bobsleigh 21

Cross purposes: lacrosse 22

Talladega nights: NASCAR 24

Rock and a hard place: rock climbing 25

South America 27

Smoke and fire: football (soccer) 28

How the other half lives: polo 30

Bare essentials: beach volleyball 31

Net gains: futevôlei (footvolley) 32

Swing and a miss: capoeira 34

Oceania 37

The home of rugby: rugby union 38

Aussie Rules: Australian Rules Football 39

Ride the wave: surfing 40

Hot shots: netball 42

Murderball: wheelchair rugby 44

Africa and the Middle East 47

Hail to the chiefs: football (soccer) 48

The long run: marathon 49

Desert duels: camel racing 50

Wing and a prayer: falconry 52

Europe 55

On the run: parkour 56

Hard as a rock: Basque stone-lifting 58

On target: darts 59

All for the craic: hurling 60

El Clásico: football (soccer) 61

The big heave: Highland Games 62

Get a grip: schwingen 64

On the rebound: pelota 65

Power and passion: Gaelic football 66

Brutality of old: Calcio Fiorentino 68

Fire and ice: biathlon 69

Four to the floor: floorball 70

All hands on deck: European handball 71

Ride of your life: cycling 72

Green with envy: golf 74

Cream of the crop: tennis 76

Leap of faith: BASE jumping 78

Flight of fancy: paragliding 79

Asia 81

The Three Manly Pursuits: Naadam 82

Get your goat: buzkashi 84

Flying high: sepak takraw 85

Getting a kick: martial arts 86

The big men fly: sumo 87

Bowled over: cricket 88

Top of the table: table tennis 90

Something in the air: jianzi 91

Taken by the horns: bull wrestling 92

On the ropes: Muay Thai 94

20 bucket-list stadiums 97

About the author 104

About the illustrator 104

Acknowledgements 105

Introduction

It almost doesn't matter what's happening on the field. It doesn't matter what the game is. It doesn't matter who's playing. Because the attraction here is sport itself.

·

It's the roar of the crowd. It's the pomp and ceremony. It's the colour and the fanfare. It's the atmosphere of tense excitement, the feeling that today could be your day, that glory could be won and victory achieved. And it's the gnawing fear, too, that none of those things might happen and you could walk away bereft.

This is sport, around the world. The highs and the lows. The passion and the pain. It's the same at La Bombonera, the incredible football stadium in the working-class suburbs of Buenos Aires, as it is at Eden Gardens, the cauldron-like cricket arena in Kolkata. It's the same at a rowdy, sweaty Muay Thai bout in suburban Bangkok as it is on a cold day at a Scottish rugby stadium.

Sport is the great leveller, the great bond between people of different backgrounds and cultures. We all understand sport. We instantly recognise the thrills and the desires. This is a universal language, one any fan can rely on wherever they are in the world, a way to tap into the local sensibility that's organic and easy and real.

For travellers, sport is the perfect lens through which to view the world. If you love sport then you love any sport. You love the celebratory atmosphere of a big event. You love the competitive nature of the games, as athletes pit their skills and their wits against each other. You love the easy camaraderie of the fans, the way you can sit there among a group of total strangers and – provided you're wearing the right colours – walk away with a whole bunch of new friends.

Through sport you can see the world and you can understand the world. It almost doesn't matter what's happening on the field.

This book is dedicated to the world of sport, some of which will be familiar to you, and some of which will not. The games and events featured in these pages vary greatly in their style and their intensity and even their popularity; however, the link between all of them is that they are genuine elements of local culture, cherished traditions that mean something to the people who participate and those who watch.

For visitors hoping to understand a little more about the place they're seeing, these sports also offer the perfect window into local life (something so vital and energising in a post-pandemic world). They're fun and they're fascinating. They're strange and they're amazing. And they're happening right now.

Game on.

Event calendar

Discover the biggest
regular sporting events
across the globe.

·

JANUARY

Australian Open, Australia
The year's first Grand Slam tennis tournament kicks off in Melbourne.

Winter X Games, USA
The best snowboarders and skiers head to Aspen, Colorado, in late January.

Tour Down Under, Australia
Australia's fledgling cycling road race takes place in South Australia.

European Men's Handball Championship, various
The venue varies year to year, but this is still the finest the game can offer (*see* p. 71).

Dakar Rally, various
The world's premier off-road endurance motor race is held in early January in various locations.

Rose Bowl Game, USA
Held on New Year's Day, this traditional NFL (National Football League) game in Los Angeles attracts huge crowds.

Grand Sumo Tournament, Japan
The first of the year's six Grand Sumo tournaments happens in Tokyo (*see* p. 87).

FEBRUARY

NBA All-Star Game, USA
The world's best basketballers take to the court for this NBA (National Basketball Association) friendly exhibition event (*see* p. 13).

Six Nations Rugby Championship, Europe
England, Wales, Scotland, Ireland, France and Italy battle it out over two months.

Super Bowl, USA

The NFL grand final is the USA's
biggest event — bucket-list stuff for
any sports fan.

Australian Grand Prix, Australia

The year's first Formula One Grand
Prix in Melbourne is always one of its
most exciting.

Tokyo Marathon, Japan

One of the world's great marathon
events takes place each March
in Tokyo.

World Table Tennis
Championships, various

The host nations for this tournament
may vary, but you can always expect
the Chinese team to dominate
(*see* p. 90).

March Madness, USA

College basketball teams line up for a
huge single-elimination tournament.

Hong Kong Sevens, China

There's always a party atmosphere
at this annual rugby sevens event.

Grand National, England

One of the world's most famous
horseraces occurs every April at
Aintree Racecourse.

The Masters, USA

Golf's finest compete at Augusta
National to wear the famous
green jacket.

MAY

Kentucky Derby, USA
The highlight of the North American horseracing calendar is run on the first Saturday in May.

Monaco Grand Prix, Monaco
Surely the most famous of the world's Grand Prix takes place on the streets of Monte Carlo.

FA Cup Final, England
The culmination of one of world football's most famous tournaments, played at Wembley Stadium.

French Open, France
This clay-court extravaganza happens at Paris's Roland Garros.

Giro d'Italia, Italy
Italy's answer to the Tour de France is a classic cycling race in its own right.

Stanley Cup Finals, USA/Canada
The final match-up of the NHL (National Hockey League) season decides who lifts the famous Stanley Cup (*see* p. 10).

Indianapolis 500, USA
Thirty-three drivers, 200 laps, 500 miles (805 kilometres) – the Indy 500 has all that and 300,000 spectators.

JUNE

UEFA Champions League Final, various
The best football players from Europe's (and, let's face it, the world's) biggest clubs battle it out.

The Championships, England
The tournament otherwise known as Wimbledon brings its pomp and ceremony to the tennis world (*see* p. 76).

24 Hours of Le Mans, France
Perhaps the world's most famous car race is a treat for both fans and drivers.

Women's PGA Championship, USA
One of women's golf's biggest prizes is decided at a different course each June.

Calcio Fiorentino, Italy

This violent version of football might be merely an exhibition sport in Florence, but it's still incredibly serious – and brutal (*see* p. 68).

(*see* p. 68)

World Muay Thai Championships, Thailand

The competition is fierce at this annual tournament held in Bangkok (*see* p. 94).

(*see* p. 94)

JULY

Summer X Games, USA

See the best skaters, BMX riders and more at this annual event held in Minneapolis.

The Open, UK

Golf's most prestigious event, the competition for the 'claret jug' occurs each July.

Naadam Festival, Mongolia

Mongolia's annual celebration of the 'Three Manly Pursuits' – wrestling, archery and horseriding – is held in the capital, Ulaanbaatar (*see* p. 82).

(*see* p. 82)

MLB All-Star Game, USA

The best players from the Major League Baseball season take to the field for an exhibition game (*see* p. 14).

(*see* p. 14)

AUGUST

Tour de France, France

One of world sport's most popular and enduring events is free for spectators to watch.

Vuelta a España, Spain

Hot on the heels of 'Le Tour', Spain's premier cycling race moves across the country in August.

Bledisloe Cup, NZ/Australia

Rugby rivalries don't get much bigger than Australia and New Zealand, who battle for the Bledisloe (*see* p. 38).

(*see* p. 38)

US Open, USA

The last of tennis's Grand Slam tournaments, held in New York City, is always exciting.

AFL Grand Final, Australia

Traditionally held on the last weekend of September, the Australian Football League's final is Aussie Rules's biggest event (*see* p. 39).

Singapore Grand Prix, Singapore

Though only a recent addition to the Grand Prix calendar, this race is already one of its best.

NBA Finals, USA

The big men take to the biggest stage for the NBA's annual finals series (*see* p. 13).

London Marathon, England

More than 40,000 runners pound London's streets during this classic endurance race.

Baseball World Series, USA

The Major League Baseball season reaches its big finale every October (*see* p. 14).

Nairobi Marathon, Kenya

See some of the finest long-distance athletes in the world at this annual race (*see* p. 49).

CAF Champions League Final, various

The culmination of the Confederation of African Football champions league tournament is always huge (*see* p. 48).

Melbourne Cup, Australia

The 'race that stops a nation' is held on the first Tuesday in November and really is a show-stopper of a horserace.

New York Marathon, USA
With more than 50,000 participants, you'll see some of the world's finest here – and plenty of others.

Argentine Open, Argentina
Argentina's premier polo event takes place before a passionate crowd (*see* p. 30).

(*see* p. 30)

DECEMBER

World Darts Championship, England
Boozy fans and dart-throwing 'athletes' head to London's 'Ally Pally' for this riotous tournament (*see* p. 59).

(*see* p. 59)

World Floorball Championships, various
The host nation of this annual tournament varies – but Sweden or Finland always wins (*see* p. 70).

(*see* p. 70)

European Women's Handball Championship, various
The finest women's handball players battle it out for supremacy in this annual event (*see* p. 71).

(*see* p. 71)

Dubai Sevens, UAE
One of the biggest events on the rugby sevens calendar takes over Dubai every December.

Boxing Day Test, Australia
Arguably the most important annual match on the world cricket calendar, played each year in Melbourne.

Sydney to Hobart, Australia
Boxing Day in Australia also marks the beginning of the famed Sydney to Hobart open-water yacht race.

Hawaiian Triple Crown of Surfing, USA
The Pipeline Masters rounds off this incredible exhibition of surfing in Hawaii.

North America

Sport: Ice hockey
See it: Canada and USA

FAST FACTS

· The Stanley Cup is named after Lord Stanley of Preston, a former governor general of Canada.

· Ice hockey games are made up of three periods of 20 minutes.

· The Montreal Canadiens is the oldest hockey team in the NHL, having been founded in 1909.

You know the old saying: I went to a fight and a game of ice hockey broke out. Yes, this is a violent sport. Surprisingly violent, in fact, given its popularity among Canadians, who must be some of the most polite people on Earth. Their sport of choice, however, is essentially UFC (Ultimate Fighting Championship) on ice, a sport of grace and beauty in some respects (huge men in full protective equipment gliding across the ice like figure skaters) and wince-inducing brutality in others. Ice hockey is fast, it's skilful and it's hardcore.

To see any NHL (National Hockey League) match in Canada or the USA is exciting. There's less of the fanfare of American football and fewer traditions than baseball. People are here for the sport and they love it. However, the culmination of the season, when the two best teams play off for the Stanley Cup, is the pinnacle, and if a Canadian team is playing then you definitely want to be there.

Ice hockey is fast, it's skilful and it's hardcore.

Sport: American football
See it: USA

You think you understand the way sports fandom works: people choose a professional team, they follow them on TV and go to games to see the best of the best play live. But then you visit the USA and realise you know nothing. Because here it's not just the big professional teams that have huge, dedicated fanbases. It's teams of college students, athletes who don't even get paid. And, even more amazingly, it's teams of high school kids who aren't even old enough to drive or vote, and yet they attract huge crowds of rabid supporters, with cheerleaders, marching bands, the whole bit.

Welcome to 'Friday Night Lights', otherwise known as high school football. To get a feel for the passion with which these minors are followed and revered, you have to get to Texas, preferably to see a home game at Lufkin High School. The Lufkin Panthers' stadium seats 10,500 fans – the town's entire population is 35,000. It's full almost every Friday night. And remember: the players here are high school students.

FAST FACTS

· The film (and TV series) *Friday Night Lights* was based on the Texas high school football team the Permian Panthers.

· American football is the second most popular high school sport in the USA (behind track and field), with over one million participants.

· The highest ever attendance for a high school football game is 54,347, at an Allen versus Pearland game in 2013.

Sport: Basketball
See it: USA

FAST FACTS

· LeBron James's teams have played in eight consecutive NBA finals, from 2011 to 2018.

· NBA athletes are the world's best-paid players by average annual salary per player.

· The LA Lakers made the NBA finals six times in the 1960s and lost to the Boston Celtics each time.

Are these the greatest athletes on the planet? You will ask yourself this every time you watch the NBA, America's national basketball league. You will ask this when you see a game on TV, for sure. And you will definitely ask it when you go to a stadium to see a game live and witness these guys up close and personal, when you stare in awe as men the size of small apartment blocks leap several feet in the air, as they pass and bounce and shoot and dunk faster than you can even see. The players in the NBA are phenomenal – their size, their skill, their power. So, are these the greatest athletes on the planet? They're certainly up there.

Though getting along to any NBA game during a trip to the USA will be a memorable occasion, perhaps the best place to watch a ballgame is the Staples Center, home of the Los Angeles Lakers, one of the NBA's perennial front-runners. The atmosphere at this 20,000-seater is always electric, and you'll be able to see the world's best in action.

THE FRIENDLY CONFINES

Sport: Baseball
See it: USA

FAST FACTS

· Wrigley Field is named after the chewing gum magnate William Wrigley Jnr, who once owned the club.

· The stadium is located in Wrigleyville, where fans stay for traditional post-game partying.

· In 2016 the Cubs won the World Series, their first since the club was 'cursed' by a local tavern owner in 1945.

You have to love a sporting stadium that is proudly nicknamed 'the Friendly Confines'. This is no 'lion's den' or 'cauldron'. And that suits Wrigley Field, the historic baseball stadium on the north side of Chicago, because the home of the Chicago Cubs really is friendly. The patrons might be the most convivial around. There's an atmosphere of celebration at every Cubs home game, as fans pack onto the old wooden benches of this more than 100-year-old stadium, pass beers and snacks down the rows to people sitting in the middle, bask in the sun, cheer their team and just generally enjoy themselves.

There are several traditions to note at Wrigley Field. One is the organ music, which is played live at every game. Another is the singing of 'Take Me Out to the Ball Game' in the middle of the seventh inning. Then you have the classic hot dogs, the hand-cranked scoreboard and the ivy-covered outfield walls. Oh, and there's a game of baseball, too, if that's your thing.

There's an atmosphere of celebration at every Cubs home game, as fans pack onto the old wooden benches of this more than 100-year-old stadium.

Sport: Curling
See it: Canada

FAST FACTS

· The Canadian men's curling team has won gold in three of the six Olympics it has participated in.

· Though it's hugely popular in Canada, it's thought curling originated in Scotland in the 16th century.

· Mixed curling, with teams of two men and two women, was introduced into the Olympics in 2018.

A sport that has famously been described as a combination of lawn bowls and housework probably doesn't sound that exciting – but then, you've never seen curling in Canada. In Canada, the humble sliding of a granite block down a sheet of ice takes on all new properties of excitement, thanks to the enthusiasm with which Canadians approach the sport. You will see this game played everywhere, from small suburban indoor centres to outdoor rinks to large purpose-built stadiums.

For those new to curling, here's how it works: in teams of four, one player slides a 20-kilogram (44-pound) granite stone down an ice 'sheet', hoping it will stop in the middle of a target at the end. Two 'sweepers' use long-handled brushes to sweep the ice in front of the stone if they want it to travel faster or straighter. Simple.

To see the sport at its finest, attend a Grand Slam of Curling 'bonspiel', or tournament, a series of four meets held across Canada.

In Canada, the humble sliding of a granite block down a sheet of ice takes on all new properties of excitement.

•

Sport: Lucha libre
See it: Mexico

FAST FACTS

· The most famous luchador of all time is 'El Santo', a silver-masked wrestler who debuted in 1942.

· Wrestlers are grouped into 'rudos', the bad guys, and 'técnicos', the good guys.

· Variations of lucha libre can also be found in Peru and Bolivia.

Mexico's most popular sport? Football. Makes sense. But how about Mexico's second most popular pastime? This particular sport is one that involves comically macho men (and sometimes women) dressed in spandex and brightly coloured masks hurling themselves at each other from great distances and great heights. It's a sport that seems to have no rules or regulations, held in a boxing ring. It's an event of huge fanfare, a manly pantomime with clearly delineated heroes and villains who are cheered and booed as their reputation befits.

The sport: lucha libre. Literal translation: free fight. Mexican wrestling has become famous worldwide thanks to the wrestlers' distinctive masks (which are only ever removed if a wrestler loses a 'lucha de apuesta', a match with a wager), their acrobatic athleticism and the sheer spectacle of the events. A lucha libre bout is a cultural rite for any visitor to Mexico and, though shows are held throughout the country, the Arena México in Mexico City is the ultimate venue, with events held three days a week.

A lucha libre bout is a cultural rite for any visitor to Mexico.

·

SKATE OR DIE

Sport: Skateboarding
See it: USA

Sport isn't always governed by rules and referees. It's not always about teams or rivalries or wearing your club colours. Sometimes sport is a little more laidback. Sometimes, sport is like skateboarding, an outsider art that hit the mainstream thanks to the likes of Tony Hawk, the X Games, and music and fashion that worked their way into popular consciousness. Skateboarding is now an Olympic sport. Its stars might still wear baggy shorts and Vans, but this is a pastime that's made it to the big time.

And if you're a fan, you have to see skating in the States. This is where Hawk is from, plus Rob Dyrdek, Ryan Sheckler and so many other great skaters. These are the world's premier exponents of the half-pipe, as well as street skating courses and mega ramps designed by the likes of Bob Burnquist. To see high-quality skateboarding in the US is as easy as heading to the park at Venice Beach in LA; or check out an X Games event or a World Skate meet; or catch one of many one-off demonstrations and events. No referees, no teams, no rivalries, no club colours. Just talented athletes having fun.

FAST FACTS

· Tony Hawk was the first skater to ever land a 900, a jump with 2.5 full spins on a half-pipe.

· American skater Danny Way has set the record for the longest jump on a skateboard: 24 metres (79 feet).

· Skateboarding as we know it was invented in Los Angeles by surfers bored when the ocean was flat.

Sport: Bobsleigh
See it: Canada

FAST FACTS

- Jamaica has now participated in bobsleigh at seven Olympic Games.

- Modern-day bobsleigh tracks are made of solid concrete coated with ice.

- The maximum weight for a competition four-man bobsleigh is 630 kilograms (1389 pounds), including crew.

Thanks to a little film called *Cool Runnings*, everyone knows what the bobsleigh is. Doesn't matter if you're from the warmest country on Earth and the idea of a 1-kilometre-long (0.6-mile-long) track of solid ice seems laughable – you still know about the bobsleigh. The famous movie about Jamaica's tilt at Olympic glory in 1988 popularised the sport the world over, even if many of us will never have the chance to actually participate.

Though, is that true? Because at Canada's Whistler Sliding Centre, one of the venues for the 2010 Winter Olympic Games, you have the chance to climb aboard a real bobsleigh and shoot down a real track, reaching speeds of up to 120 kilometres (74 miles) per hour, and pulling about 5 g in terms of g-force. This is the Passenger Bobsleigh Experience, in which three paying customers get to act as crew for a professional driver, crouching in the back of a bobsleigh and hanging on as the carriage whips through turn after turn, getting faster and faster as it roars down the hill.

Doesn't matter where you're from – you now have a bobsleigh team.

Sport: Lacrosse
See it: Canada and USA

FAST FACTS

· Lacrosse can be played outdoors or in a six-person indoor format called box lacrosse.

· Outdoor lacrosse was a medal sport in the 1904 and 1908 Olympic Games.

· Lacrosse is a popular women's sport – the first US team was established in 1926.

Most of the USA's most popular sports have made it big on the world stage. You might not play baseball, but you know about it. Same goes for basketball. And even NFL. But lacrosse? Not too many people outside of North America know much about lacrosse. And yet in its homeland it is phenomenally popular, and is in fact the oldest organised sport in both Canada and the USA.

Lacrosse is based on games played by Native American communities as far back as a thousand years ago, games that were later documented by missionaries and explorers, and that eventually became the sport we know as lacrosse during the 1800s. The game was first popularised in Canada (and you will see great games there), but is now one of the fastest-growing team sports in the USA.

Lacrosse is part hockey, part netball: two teams of ten players, each armed with sticks with a small basket on the end, attack a goal; certain players have to stay in certain zones of the field. The winning team is the one with the most goals at the end. There are several professional men's and women's lacrosse leagues in North America, the biggest of which is probably the Major League Lacrosse.

Lacrosse is based on games played by Native American communities.

TALLADEGA NIGHTS

Sport: NASCAR
See it: USA

NASCAR racing is about many things,
but mostly it's about speed. These races
are held on oval-shaped tracks with
few avenues for tricky manoeuvring
or complex team tactics. Instead, cars
just drive really, really fast. And the fans
love it. To soak up the passion and the
fanfare of NASCAR, you have to head
to its heartland: Talladega Speedway in
Lincoln, Alabama. Up to 175,000 rabid
fans can squeeze into this phenomenal
venue, which at 4.28 kilometres
(2.66 miles) long is NASCAR's
longest track. It's also its fastest,
with NASCAR's record top speed of
348 kilometres (216 miles) per hour hit
at Talladega by Rusty Wallace in 2004.

So there you have it: big, fast and a lot of fun.
A race meet at Talladega is a whole festival of
revhead action; weekend meets involve several
races and include camping on-site, plus all
the beer and hotdogs you can carry. For true
fans – or for those who visit when there's no
race meet on – there's also the chance to do a
Driving Experience, getting behind the wheel of a
NASCAR vehicle and being let loose on the track.
It is, as they say at Talladega, as real as it gets.

FAST FACTS

· NASCAR legend Dale
  Earnhardt holds the
  record for the most
  wins at Talladega,
  with ten.

· Talladega Speedway
  is rumoured to be
  cursed after a string
  of untimely deaths at
  the track.

· Talladega is a tight
  circuit known for its
  multi-car crashes,
  which are called
  'the Big One'.

Sport: Rock climbing
See it: USA

FAST FACTS

· Alex Honnold ascended the 900-metre (3000-foot) face of El Capitan in just under four hours. With no ropes.

· Tom Cruise insisted on doing his own stunts in *Mission: Impossible 2* – that's really him on that rock face.

· Ancient Chinese artworks show people rock climbing as far back as 200BCE.

There are two iconic moments for rock climbing on film. One is the opening scene for *Mission: Impossible 2*, in which Tom Cruise clings to a cliff-face high in the air, without even a rope to hold him. That, of course, was fake (Cruise was doing the climbing but he had safety wires). The other is *Free Solo*, in which Alex Honnold clings to a cliff-face high in the air, without even a rope to hold him. That was real. Cruise is an actor. Honnold is a freakish climber who has scaled the famous El Capitan in Yosemite National Park without ropes or harness.

Both of those filmic moments capture not just the drama and skill of rock climbing, but also a few iconic locations within the USA for those who like to scale big rocks. Cruise was in Moab, a small town in Utah that attracts the world's best climbers. Honnold was at El Cap, probably the world's most famous climbing venue. The USA has an embarrassment of world-class venues for climbers of all skill levels, from beginner-friendly Red Rock in Nevada to the challenging likes of Devils Tower in Wyoming. Just remember: bring ropes.

South America

Sport: Football (soccer)
See it: Argentina

FAST FACTS

· The official capacity of La Bombonera is 49,000, though its highest recorded attendance is just over 57,000 fans.

· The stadium's nickname means 'the chocolate box', owing to its unique shape.

· La Bombonera plays host to the intense rivalry of the Superclásico, between Boca and River Plate.

This is it: the pinnacle of football fandom. As wild and exciting as it gets. Nowhere will you find fans as raucous packed into a stadium as intimidating. Nowhere will you be so enthralled and so amazed.

This is La Bombonera, home to Argentina's Boca Juniors football club. The experience of seeing a game here is intense from the moment you step into the working-class neighbourhood of La Boca. The stadium, also known as Estadio Alberto J. Armando, sits in the centre of the suburb, amid houses and bars within touching distance of its graffiti-covered walls. The arena itself reflects that closeness, with stands crowding a pitch that's the smallest permissible by FIFA.

La Bombonera's atmosphere is electric, almost overwhelming. This is an entire stadium of hardcore fans, known as 'La Doce', or the 12th player, a roiling sea of yellow and blue that dances and shouts and cheers and screams, with umbrellas twirling and drums beating and lit firecrackers being hurled. You'll see fans here scale the high fences that surround the pitch and tie themselves to the top. You'll see smoke from flares. You'll see, amid the chaos, amid the insanity, a game of football. There's nowhere else like it.

You'll see smoke from flares. You'll see, amid the chaos, amid the insanity, a game of football.

Sport: Polo
See it: Argentina

South America: it's all passion and flair, right? It's the roar of football fans, the chaos of the political scene, the love of good food. It's the unique cultures of Indigenous peoples mixed with the influence of the Spanish, Italians and Portuguese.

All of that is correct. And yet polo is popular. Polo, the sport of the English gentry. Polo, the game for the rich. Polo, aka hockey on horseback. It's huge in Argentina, with its links to British culture – particularly in Buenos Aires, which feels like a small part of Europe transported. Here, polo is approached with as much passion and fervour as any other pastime.

Polo's heartland is in the Buenos Aires neighbourhoods of Belgrano and Palermo, traditionally some of the city's wealthiest locales, home of the Argentine Polo Association and the Campo Argentino del Polo field. The annual pinnacle is La Triple Corona, a series of three tournaments that runs from September to the end of the year. To see the passion that bubbles away on the field and in the stands is something to behold.

FAST FACTS

- The three tournaments of La Triple Corona are the Tortugas Open, the Hurlingham Open and the Argentine Open.

- The most successful local team is La Dolfina, founded by local polo superstar Adolfo Cambiaso.

- Polo players must hold their mallet in their right hand, regardless of natural preference.

Sport: Beach volleyball
See it: Brazil, Chile, Venezuela

FAST FACTS

- The sport of beach volleyball began in Hawaii in 1915, at the Outrigger Canoe Club on Waikiki Beach.

- Brazilian pairs have won gold at the Olympic Games three times; that's second only to the USA with six.

- The official uniforms for beach volleyball players are bikinis for women, and shorts no longer than 20 centimetres (7 inches) above the knees for men.

Beach volleyball is popular around the world for a variety of reasons: it's skilful, it's athletic, you get to watch it at the beach, and the players involved tend to be, shall we say, not hard on the eye. This is a sport with a whole lot going for it, though to see it in the flesh is to truly appreciate just how talented the game's professionals tend to be.

As you could probably have guessed, beach volleyball is popular in Brazil. All of those huge beaches, all of those athletically gifted locals. It makes sense (though both Chile and Venezuela also excel). In Brazil you'll see the game being played on the likes of Copacabana and Ipanema beaches in Rio de Janeiro, Cabo Branco in João Pessoa, Pajuçara in Maceió and, perhaps most importantly of all, at the sprawling Camburi Beach in Espiritu Santo. Plenty of Brazil's major beach volleyball tournaments are played at Camburi, and on any given sunny day you will catch some of the sport's premier exponents strutting their stuff on the warm sand. If you're lucky you might even be asked to join a game (though, not with the professionals).

Sport: Futevôlei (footvolley)
See it: Brazil

FAST FACTS

- Futevôlei was created by Octávio de Moraes in 1965, at Copacabana in Rio de Janeiro.

- Brazilian football stars Ronaldo, Ronaldinho and Romário are regular futevôlei players.

- There's a European Footvolley League – the top-ranked team, unsurprisingly, is Portugal.

If you ever wanted proof that Brazilians are the greatest natural footballers on the planet, just head down to the beach. Specifically, head to a Rio de Janeiro beach such as Copacabana or Ipanema and cast your eye over the beach volleyball courts, where plenty of people will be playing a game that's at its most popular in Brazil: futevôlei, or footvolley. Why is this game best loved in Brazil? Probably because it's too hard for everyone else. This is a game of volleyball in which you're not allowed to use your hands. It's all of the skills of football – kicking a ball, controlling it on your chest, using your head, thighs or even shoulders to propel the ball – applied to volleyball.

It is spectacular to watch and very difficult to play. Don't even try to get involved – you'll be embarrassed. Simply sit back at a beachside kiosk with a caipirinha and watch these athletes in action as they show such incredible control of the football, volleying it back and forth over a high net. If they're this good on sand, with a huge net in front of them, imagine how good they are on a football pitch.

It is spectacular to watch and very difficult to play.

Sport: Capoeira
See it: Brazil

FAST FACTS

· Capoeira was declared illegal in Brazil when slavery was abolished in the late 1800s, and only became legal again in the 1930s.

· The sport is often accompanied by people playing the berimbau, a single-stringed instrument.

· Capoeira is performed in a 'roda', a circle formed by other players and musicians.

Is this a sport or a dance? Is it a martial art or a show? With capoeira it's sometimes difficult to tell, and that's part of the attraction for its many exponents in Brazil. Capoeira is the perfect snapshot of Brazilian culture and history, a pastime with roots in African slavery, inextricably linked to local passions such as music and dance. To see capoeira is to witness a joyful flow of movement, as two 'capoeiristas' face off against each other and engage in a series of high kicks and low sweeps, as they feint and weave, dodge and duck, all the while accompanied by musicians and other performers. The capoeiristas rarely make physical contact: this is a game of skill, rather than one designed to inflict pain.

You'll see capoeira being practised throughout Brazil; however, the coastal city of Salvador, with its indelible ties to the African slave trade and its strong modern-day Afro-Brazilian culture, is considered the home of capoeira, and the ideal place to witness capoeiristas in action. In Pelourinho, the old town of Salvador, several iconic capoeira schools put on displays (for tips) on the cobbled streets. Bring your camera.

Capoeira is the perfect snapshot of Brazilian culture and history.

·

Oceania

THE HOME OF RUGBY

Sport: Rugby union
See it: New Zealand

No one loves rugby like the Kiwis do. No one. And in a not unrelated fact, no one is as good at rugby as those from the Land of the Long White Cloud. This is a nation of fewer than five million people, and yet the All Blacks, the New Zealand rugby team, is undisputedly the best in the world, with three World Cup wins out of nine tournaments for the men, and five World Cup wins out of eight for the women. Kiwis live and breathe rugby. The happiness of the nation rests upon the shoulders of the 15 men or women tasked with representing them on the rugby field.

Go to any match in New Zealand, from high school games to provincial championships, and you will see the passion for the game on display. But go to 'the Cauldron' – otherwise known as Eden Park in Auckland – and you will see fandom at its most passionate, and rugby at its most brutal and beautiful. Go to Eden Park to see a Bledisloe Cup game, meanwhile, to see the All Blacks take on their arch rivals Australia, and you will see something else entirely. The game they play in heaven, rugby fans like to say. For the All Blacks, they're already there.

FAST FACTS

· New Zealand won the first ever Rugby World Cup, in 1987. It would take them 24 years to win another.

· New Zealand has won the Bledisloe Cup 47 times; Australia, just 12.

· The Kiwi rugby team is called the All Blacks; the nation's basketball team is the Tall Blacks.

Sport: Australian Rules Football
See it: Australia

Australians go mad for Aussie Rules,
or AFL, the unique local sport that's
a little like Ireland's Gaelic football, a
little like America's NFL and a little like
nothing else you've ever seen before.
Two teams of 18 players gather on an
oval-shaped field and attempt to boot
an egg-shaped ball through a set of
four goalposts located at each end. The
result is a fast, athletic, acrobatic and
at times brutal game that sets the local
pulses racing, particularly if you happen
to find yourself in the states of Victoria,
South Australia and Western Australia.

However, that's not where the nation's most
exciting game is played. For real footy fandom,
you have to get to the Tiwi Islands, off the coast
of far northern Australia. Here you will witness
grand final weekend for the Tiwi Islands football
league, where crowds of up to 3000 people –
more than the islands' entire population – gather
to see their best and brightest fight it out for
glory. This is no-frills footy, fuelled by pure
passion, and the atmosphere is amazing.

Sport: Surfing
See it: Australia

FAST FACTS

· Surfing was introduced into Australia by Hawaiian legend Duke Kahanamoku in 1915.

· Australians Stephanie Gilmore and Layne Beachley have each won the world title seven times.

· Of Australia's population of 25 million, 2.5 million identify as surfers.

Take a look at the list of past world surfing champions: Australia has had 20 winners in the men's competition's 56 years of existence; and 23 in the 52 years of the women's comp. That's a third of the men's winners and almost half of the women. Australians love to surf and they're good at it. Along with California and Hawaii, this is one of the homes of surfing, a country where pretty much any beach with a decent wave will be filled with the bobbing shapes of chilled-out surfers on boards, waiting for the next ride.

There are so many iconic waves here. Check out Bells Beach, home of the Rip Curl Pro, and setting for that iconic final scene in *Point Break*. Check out Margaret River, a series of stunningly beautiful surf beaches amid Western Australian wine country. And don't forget the Gold Coast in Queensland, home to Snapper Rocks, Duranbah, Burleigh Heads and the Superbank. Slap on some sunscreen and get out there – or, alternatively, find a good spot on the sand and watch some of the world's best.

Australians love to surf and they're good at it.

.

Sport: Netball
See it: New Zealand

FAST FACTS

· Netball is played by more than 20 million people in over 80 countries.

· This is an adapted version of basketball and became its own sport in 1901.

· Fast5 is an altered version of netball that involves five-player teams and shorter games.

If you know anything about sport in New Zealand, then you know rugby is popular. Seriously popular. And yet, as far as people who actually play the game are concerned – particularly for school-age kids – rugby is not the top tier in New Zealand. That crown goes to netball, which has the highest participation among young New Zealanders, and is also a phenomenally popular professional sport, with large crowds turning out to see the Silver Ferns, the New Zealand national side, as well as a slew of provincial teams. You'll read about netball on the back page of the paper in New Zealand. You'll hear games being spoken about in cafes. This is a fast, athletic and skilful game, and it's a big deal.

To see the country's best in action, you have several options, including catching an ANZ Premiership game, the top rung of the domestic competition; seeing a match-up in the Super Cup, an end-of-year competition featuring some of the best clubs in the world; or getting along to see the Silver Ferns. If the national side is playing Australia, bask in the sport's biggest rivalry.

You'll read about netball on the back page of the paper in New Zealand.

MURDERBALL

Sport: Wheelchair rugby
See it: Australia

FAST FACTS

· The wheelchair rugby documentary *Murderball* was voted the Number One Sports Movie of All Time by Rotten Tomatoes.

· Wheelchair rugby games are played over four eight-minute quarters. Teams can have up to 12 members.

· The sport was invented for those who couldn't play wheelchair basketball because of upper-limb impairments.

If you think rugby is brutal, wait until you see the game played in wheelchairs. This is a sport that has been nicknamed 'murderball' thanks to the passion and occasional violence of its exponents. Physical contact is very much allowed in wheelchair rugby.

Two teams of four people – a mix of men and women, all wheelchair-bound through disability – line up against each other on an indoor area the size of a basketball court. The idea, as with rugby, is to get the ball from one end and score a try down the other. The players themselves can't touch each other; however, their wheelchairs definitely can.

Wheelchair rugby was created in Canada in 1976, though it quickly gained popularity in Australia, where outdoor rugby has long been a passion. Australia won silver the first year wheelchair rugby was included in the Paralympic Games, in 2000, and has won gold in 2012 and 2016. It's not always possible to catch a game live, but it's worth checking the schedule any time you're in Sydney, the national team's base.

Physical contact is very much allowed in wheelchair rugby.

.

Africa and the
Middle East

HAIL TO THE CHIEFS

Sport: Football (soccer)
See it: South Africa

You may have heard of the English rock band the Kaiser Chiefs – but they weren't the originals. The first and finest were the Kaizer Chiefs, a South African football club based in Soweto, the sprawling township just outside Johannesburg. As far as African club football goes, the Chiefs live up to their name: they've won the South African national league 12 times, South Africa's cup tournament 41 times and the African Cup Winners' Cup once. They're also sub-Saharan Africa's most popular club.

The biggest match for the Kaizer Chiefs in any given season is the Soweto Derby, a game against cross-town rivals the Orlando Pirates. These matches are played at FNB Stadium, the 95,000-seat arena otherwise known as 'the Calabash', and the atmosphere is electric, raucous and very, very noisy. The Chiefs have the edge on the Pirates, with 31 wins to 16.

FAST FACTS

- The English band named themselves the Kaiser Chiefs because the captain of their own favourite club, Leeds United, once played for the South Africans.

- The Kaizer Chiefs are named after their founder, Kaizer Motaung.

- FNB Stadium was the site of Nelson Mandela's first formal speech after release from prison in 1990.

Sport: Marathon
See it: Kenya

FAST FACTS

· Kenyan runner Eliud Kipchoge is the only person to have ever run a marathon in under two hours (1 hour, 59 minutes and 40 seconds to be exact).

· The winner of the first ever Olympic marathon was Greek runner Spyridon Louis, in 1896.

· The first ever Olympic women's marathon wasn't staged until 1984.

Kenyans can run. You don't need to be told that. Close your eyes and you can easily picture that iconic black-and-red singlet at the Olympic Games, as Kenyans breast the tape in any of the middle- or long-distance events. Together with those athletes of neighbouring Ethiopia, the Kenyans can regularly be found on the podium, and indeed Kenyans won gold in both the men's and women's marathons at the 2016 Olympics. Kenyans. Can. Run.

So you can imagine the fanfare involved at the nation's premier distance running event, the Nairobi Marathon. The event has been held since 2003, and it's serious business. This isn't a fun-run. It's not the sort of event that attracts tens of thousands of entrants. No one wears fancy dress. They're here to race, to punch out 42 kilometres (26 miles) through the streets of the Kenyan capital in the fastest time possible. And Kenyan athletes have won both the men's and women's competitions every year. You know why that is.

AFRICA AND THE MIDDLE EAST

Sport: Camel racing
See it: UAE

FAST FACTS

- Robot jockeys were introduced in 2001, when the UAE banned the use of child jockeys.

- These robot jockeys have a whipping arm, as well as a GPS and heartrate sensor.

- Racing camels can run at speeds of up to 65 kilometres (40 miles) an hour.

First thing you're probably going to ask yourself about camel racing in Dubai is: what the hell is going on here? There's a lot to take in. There's the sight of the camels themselves, these somehow beautiful beasts that are treated as royalty by their owners (who might be actual royalty). Then there are the jockeys – not actual people, but small boxes strapped to the camels' backs. Then there's the size of the track itself, which seems to stretch past the horizon. And then there's the fleet of luxury cars poised trackside, ready to roll.

What's going on here is Emirati camel racing. The animals themselves are highly prized. The robot jockeys on their backs are controlled remotely by trainers riding in cars nearby. The track is 10 kilometres (6 miles) long – owners and trainers follow the animals in luxury SUVs. Even some spectators can follow the camels in mini-buses. There will be plenty of commotion at the finish, particularly in a prestigious race such as the annual championship at Al Marmoum racetrack, just outside Dubai. And the best thing of all? Entrance is free.

> There's the sight of the camels themselves, these somehow beautiful beasts that are treated as royalty by their owners.

Sport: Falconry
See it: UAE

FAST FACTS

· Peregrine falcons can fly at speeds up to 390 kilometres (242 miles) per hour – they're the fastest members of the animal kingdom.

· Falcons in the UAE are usually trained to hunt houbara bustards, curlews and hares.

· A top-quality falcon can sell for up to AU$40,000 (about US$30,000).

If you ever find yourself in the first-class cabin of an Emirates or Etihad flight in the Middle East, cast your eye around for falcons. Yes, the birds. Falconry is a popular sport among royals and other high-society types in Dubai and Abu Dhabi, and they often need to transport their birds to various events. So important are falcons to the Emiratis that they're the only animals allowed to fly in the plane's main cabin; they also have their own passports.

There's a rich tradition in the Emirates of falconry, the practice of training a bird – usually a Saker or Peregrine falcon – to hunt prey and return it to its owner. To see the sport live is quite phenomenal: the beauty, the speed and the power of the falcons, the grace with which they fly through the air, the brutality of the kill. Though true falconry – including the hunt and kill – is rare to witness in the UAE, most cultural demonstrations and desert safaris include watching a trained falcon fly and return to its trainer. It's also possible to visit the Abu Dhabi Falcon Hospital, where injured birds are cared for and rehabilitated.

To see the sport live is quite phenomenal: the beauty, the speed and the power of the falcons.

.

Europe

Sport: Parkour
See it: France

FAST FACTS

· Frenchman David Belle is considered to have founded the sport of parkour in the 1990s.

· The name comes from the French word 'parcours', meaning course.

· Though competitive events involving parkour exist, there are no set rules or regulations for the sport.

When you think about it, this is the simplest sport imaginable: there's no equipment, no teams, no organisation, no actual rules. Parkour utilises the surrounding environment and requires nothing but a pair of shoes and a fair amount of daring. You just take to the streets and run, jump, climb and crawl.

Parkour has its roots in France, which is still the sport's most important base, though the practice of running and jumping through an urban environment has links to military obstacle-course training, and had been taking place in some form throughout the world before it became recognised as a pursuit in France. But here it's at its most popular; here, on the streets of Paris and Marseilles, Le Mans and Lyon, you're most likely to see groups of people leaping off buildings and balancing on railings, climbing high walls and vaulting over obstacles.

There are no organised competitions, no scheduled meets. No rules. No teams. Just hang around the right spots and wait for the athletes to appear.

There are no
organised
competitions,
no scheduled
meets. No
rules.

HARD AS A ROCK

Sport: Basque stone-lifting
See it: Spain

Surely not. Surely that guy is not going to be able to lift that rock. It weighs 150 kilograms (330 pounds). No one could do that. But then, he does lift that rock. He grapples with it, flipping the huge stone onto his knees, bracing as he hauls it up to his chest and onto his shoulder. A referee yells and he drops the stone to the floor with a crash. And then ... he picks it up again. And again.

Welcome to the sport of harri-jasotze, or Basque stone-lifting. This is a rural sport practised in the mountains of northern Spain, in the Basque Country, where the language is different, the food is different and the pastimes are different. There are numerous rural sports local to this area, but stone-lifting is the most popular, where big men gather to pick up huge rocks – sometimes cube-shaped, sometimes cylindrical, others roughly hewn and natural – and try to hoist them onto their shoulders as many times as possible within a set time limit.

The best place to see the lifters is in the seaside holiday town of San Sebastián, during Euskal Jaiak, the Basque Festival. Join the cider-sipping crowds in Plaza Trinidad and marvel at the big men doing their thing.

FAST FACTS

- The sport's name is built on the Basque words 'harri' for stone and 'jaso', to lift.

- The preferred stone for the sport is harri beltza, a local black granite.

- Mieltxo Saralegi holds the record for the heaviest stone every lifted: 329 kilograms (725 pounds).

FAST FACTS

· Englishman Phil 'The Power' Taylor has won the World Darts Championship (WDC) a record 14 times.

· A perfect game of darts involves scoring 501 in just nine throws. It's been done nine times at the WDC.

· In 2015 Phil Taylor was rated by the BBC as one of the ten greatest British sportsmen of the last 35 years.

Sport: Darts
See it: England

Somehow, at some point, darts became fun. In fact, not just fun, but a riotously good time. Somehow the World Darts Championship, held each year at London's Alexandra Palace – aka the 'Ally Pally' – became *the* social event for sports-loving English people who enjoy mixing fancy dress and copious amounts of alcohol with their consumption of the big game. And so, this sport that features everyday men and women throwing tiny arrows at a circular target has morphed into a cultural phenomenon, a date as important as any football match or cricket game.

Here's how it works. You score tickets for you and your mates to a day at the Ally Pally. Preferably grand final day, though really any date will work. You decide on your group's fancy dress theme – maybe Telly Tubbies, or superheroes or Hawaiian shirts or you all dress as giant beer bottles. Then you get along to the darts, you drink, you sing songs, you write messages on pieces of cardboard and try to get them on television, you drink some more, and at some point a few games of darts happen. Wouldn't miss it for the world.

ALL FOR THE CRAIC

Sport: Hurling
See it: Ireland

This is not a game for the faint-hearted. Hurling is fast, skilful and tough. It's an Irish game featuring two teams of 15 players, all armed with 'hurls', or long wooden sticks with broad, flat bases. The players are all chasing a 'sliotar', a small, leather-covered ball, which they're trying to get either into or over the top of a goal at each end of the field. The players can shoulder charge others holding the ball. That ball, with a good strike of a hurl, can travel at speeds of up to 150 kilometres (93 miles) per hour. No one wears any pads. Helmets were only made compulsory in 2010.

You don't have to understand hurling to enjoy it. All you need is appreciation for the 'craic', that distinctly Irish love of good company and a good time. To attend a hurling match in Ireland is to join a cherished cultural tradition, to yell yourself hoarse cheering on the local team, to enjoy the spectacle, and to head off to a local pub at the end of the game for a Guinness or three. The country's biggest competition is the All-Ireland Senior Championship, and a trip to Dublin's Croke Park for the final should be on every sporting bucket list.

FAST FACTS

· The All-Ireland final has been played at Croke Park every year but two since 1910.

· With a capacity of 82,300, Croke Park is the third largest stadium in Europe.

· The first official rules for hurling were established in 1884.

EL CLÁSICO

Sport: Football (soccer)
See it: Spain

FAST FACTS

· The largest margin in a Clásico is the 11–1 thumping Real dealt to Barcelona in 1943.

· The top goal-scorer in the Clásico's history is Barça superstar Lionel Messi.

· The highest ever attendance was 120,000 people in Barcelona in 1989.

There are plenty of great sporting rivalries in Europe, particularly when it comes to football: Arsenal and Tottenham; Rangers and Celtic; Roma and Lazio; Partizan Belgrade and Red Star. However, perhaps none reach the heights – in terms of star power, pomp and sheer size – of Spain's Clásico, the match-up between Real Madrid and Barcelona. These two powerhouse clubs are diametrically opposed. One is from the capital, one from the separatists. One is rich, known as 'Los Millionarios', the other is proudly owned by its fans. One will do whatever it takes to win, the other likes to say it plays the beautiful game.

It doesn't matter which you prefer. What matters is that you get along to a game at the Santiago Bernabéu in Madrid or Camp Nou in Barcelona and you see these two greats battle it out on the pitch. The teams are almost impossible to split: they've played each other at least twice a year since 1929 and the spoils are pretty much even. The only certainty is that you will see some of the best players in the world in one of the most important matches of their careers.

THE BIG HEAVE

Sport: Highland Games
See it: Scotland

FAST FACTS

· The world's largest Highland Games, by attendance, is actually held each year in Pleasanton, California.

· The oldest Highland Games meet is held in the Scottish village of Ceres.

· The caber, the log used in caber tossing, typically weighs about 80 kilograms (176 pounds).

It's not often you have the chance to watch a large, red-headed man in a kilt throw a log the size of a telephone pole in the air, but welcome to the Scottish Highland Games, where such a sight is commonplace. Caber tossing is just one of the events at this celebration of ancient Scottish and Celtic tradition; the sport involves a competitor holding a long, heavy log upright in their hands, and then attempting to flip it, tossing the log in such a way that it turns end over end. It's more difficult than it sounds.

Other events at a classic Highland Games include hammer-throwing, tossing a weighted stone over a bar, and throwing a 'sheaf' (a bundle of straw). These competitions are usually accompanied by traditional music – played on the bagpipes, obviously – as well as dancing and, occasionally, a little drinking. The games take place across Scotland throughout spring and summer, though the largest meet is the Cowal Highland Gathering, held in Dunoon every August. Expect friendly crowds, a celebratory atmosphere and big men in tartan.

> **Expect friendly crowds, a celebratory atmosphere and big men in tartan.**
>
> •

Sport: Schwingen
See it: Switzerland

It begins with a solemn prayer. The competitors gather high on an alp in the rich green hills of Switzerland and pause respectfully as Sunday mass is observed and the choir sings hymns. And then it's time to wrestle.

This is schwingen, traditional Swiss wrestling. It's little known throughout the rest of the world, and yet perennially popular and passionately revered in its homeland. This is a rural sport, a sport for farmers, for workers, for strapping lads in checked shirts who gather on these beautiful alps, don the wrestlers' traditional hessian trousers (known as 'schwingerhosen'), enter sawdust-covered rings and then attempt to throw each other to the ground. As soon as your shoulders hit the sawdust, you've lost. The victor brushes the dust from the vanquished. They move on.

As ever, it's the action outside the ring that's as exciting as the sport itself. Most schwingen meets in Switzerland involve beer and sausages, a few casual bets and plenty of time in the sun, chatting and enjoying the views.

FAST FACTS

- Though it's an ancient sport, schwingen's modern history can be traced to a festival in 1805.

- Women participate; the Women's Schwingen Association was founded in 1992.

- Winners of major schwingen tournaments are traditionally awarded a bull.

Sport: Pelota
See it: Spain, France

Look around any town in northern Spain or south-western France, no matter how big or small, and you will find a 'fronton', or pelota court. It's usually just a big wall in front of an open area, set near apartment blocks and shops, beside bars and restaurants. The fronton is part of the city, because pelota is part of life.

This is a game traditionally played by the Basques of Spain and France, though its popularity has spread through Latin America, the Philippines and the USA. It's a sport that takes many forms, each of which involves a ball and a wall. Depending on the discipline, that ball can be struck with the hand, or it can be hit with a 'pala corta', a short wooden bat, or a 'pala larga', a larger bat. There's also a large basket, known as a 'cesta punta', which is used to hurl the ball for the pelota variation, 'jai alai'.

Whichever form the game takes, pelota is a deeply respected tradition in the Basque Country, one that's passed down through families — the children of past champions are expected to excel at the game — and one you will see practised in the frontons in any town you happen to visit.

FAST FACTS

- The ball in jai alai has been clocked as fast as 302 kilometres (187 miles) per hour.

- Mexicans play a hybrid game of pelota and tennis called frontenis.

- Spain has won the most Basque Pelota World Championships medals, followed by France and Mexico.

Sport: Gaelic football
See it: Ireland

FAST FACTS

- Kerry is the most successful county in Ireland, with 37 championship victories since 1888.

- Teams are awarded three points for hitting the lower part of the goal and one point for the higher section.

- A hybrid game called International Rules has been developed to allow Ireland to play against Australia's AFL players.

This is one of those sports you might never have seen before, and yet you will instantly understand. Gaelic football is a hybrid of sports and skills that any fan would recognise. It's similar to soccer, played using a round ball on a rectangular pitch with goals at each end. It's reminiscent of rugby, in that you can use hands and feet, and the goals stretch high into the air. And it's a lot like any sport, especially in Ireland, in that it features huge crowds of passionate fans who love both their team and a beer afterwards.

The top tier of Gaelic football in Ireland is the All-Ireland Championship, a knockout competition featuring teams representing each of Ireland's counties, with the two finalists meeting at the end of the season at Dublin's Croke Park. Though the final is the big one, it's actually just as good to see a match in any county, at any stadium, to soak up the passion of both players and fans, to watch for the big hits, to cheer for the local team, and to toast victory or drown sorrows in the pub afterwards.

It features huge crowds of passionate fans who love both their team and a beer afterwards.

Sport: Calcio Fiorentino
See it: Italy

Is this a sport or a riot? Sometimes you won't know. Maybe it's both. The only thing for certain is that Calcio Fiorentino (also known as Calcio Storico) is not for the timid. Not even for the sane. This game, played only in Florence in Italy, is a very early form of football, thought to have originated in the 1500s. And it is, in a word, brutal. Stunningly, unbelievably brutal.

The aim is for teams of 27 players to get a ball from their end of a rectangular field to a goal at the other end. Standing in their way: 27 players from the opposing team, who can do whatever they want to stop them – punching, kicking, tripping, head-butting, tackling, wrestling. The only moves that are banned are 'sucker punches' from behind and kicking in the head. Everything else is fair.

There are only four teams in Florence, representing the city's most important neighbourhoods. They wear four colours: red, white, light blue and green. The players compete in just one tournament a year, held to coincide with the Feast of San Giovanni, the patron saint of Florence, on 24 June. The players wear the traditional pantaloons of old. They face each other in a fenced-off arena. And they go to town.

FAST FACTS
- Calcio Fiorentino originated in the 15th century – even popes played the game.

- The game was reintroduced in Italy in 1930 by Benito Mussolini.

- The winning team receives a free dinner; the losers get nothing.

Sport: Biathlon
See it: Austria

FAST FACTS

- Biathlon first began as a military training exercise in Norway in the 1700s.

- Biathlon involves two shooting positions in each race: standing and lying prone.

- Missed targets in the shooting discipline result in time penalties or extra ski distance.

It's not hard to figure out the origins of the sport of biathlon: this is a mix of cross-country skiing and shooting, the necessary skill set for anyone hoping to survive in the north of Europe in the days of old. Skiing, shooting – you get it. This seemingly simple sport, however, is deceptively difficult, with athletes having to master two very different disciplines, as well as master their own bodies as they transition from hardcore cross-country skiing into the calm and stillness necessary for accurate shooting.

To so many people born outside of this part of the world, biathlon can seem entirely theoretical. When would you have the chance to do either cross-country skiing or rifle shooting, let alone combine them? The good news, however, is that this legendary sport is available to rank amateurs on a visit to Austria. In the Tirol region, the Nordic centres in Hochfilzen, Obertilliach, Seefeld and Erpfendorf all hold regular classes in winter, introducing beginners to biathlon. Ski fast, shoot straight.

FOUR TO THE FLOOR

Sport: Floorball
See it: Sweden

At first glance, floorball seems like little more than training for ice hockey when the weather isn't cold enough. And that's how it began. Played on an indoor rink similar in size to hockey, floorball players use sticks to propel a ball to each other and into a goal. Only, there's no ice. What started as a training exercise, however, has morphed into a seriously popular sport, particularly in Sweden, where floorball players are national stars and professional domestic competition is fierce.

Get to a Swedish Super League match – there are 14-club men's and women's competitions played across the country – and bear witness to the seriousness with which this sport is taken. The crowds are raucous and the gameplay is lightning fast. The best players will represent Sweden in the World Floorball Championship, a tournament the Scandinavian nation has won eight out of 12 times.

FAST FACTS

· Floorball teams are made up of six players, including one goalkeeper.

· The game began in Canada, but was turned into a competitive sport in Sweden in the 1970s.

· Only two teams have ever won the men's World Floorball Championship: Sweden and Finland.

Sport: European handball
See it: Denmark

FAST FACTS

· Handball teams have seven players on court and seven subs, and play two 30-minute halves.

· Players in possession of the ball can take three steps and hold the ball for three seconds.

· The highest attendance at a handball game was 44,189 at the Waldstadion in Frankfurt, in 2014.

Here's another sport that might be unfamiliar to many outside Europe, and yet is instantly understandable. Two teams – either men or women – line up on an indoor court. There are goals at each end. The players use their hands to pass a small ball around, with the hope of scoring a goal at the other end. So far, so simple. And that's pretty much European handball. This is not an overly complicated game. It is, however, a fast game and a thrilling game, with the ball flying from hand to hand, players diving and sliding to make their shots, and scores regularly high.

As the name suggests, this is a European game popular across the continent, though more so in the north. It was first codified in Denmark, and the Danes remain highly competitive, having won gold in the men's competition at the 2016 Rio Olympics, and winning the 2019 World Men's Handball Championship. The women's team won gold at three Olympics in a row. There are men's and women's professional handball leagues in Denmark, playing 26-match seasons around the country – which means, in a place the size of Denmark, you're never far from a game.

Sport: Cycling
See it: France

FAST FACTS

- The first Tour was held in 1903 to increase sales for the main sponsor, *L'Auto* newspaper.

- *L'Auto* was printed on yellow paper, hence the winner's jersey is yellow.

- Four riders share the record for having won the Tour five times. They are Jacques Anquetil, Eddy Merckx, Bernard Hinault and Miguel Indurain.

There might be no greater sporting event in the world than the Tour de France. The sheer athleticism of these cyclists is phenomenal: they ride almost 3500 kilometres (just over 2000 miles) in three weeks, climbing huge mountains, negotiating white-knuckle descents and maintaining average speeds of around 40 kilometres (24 miles) per hour. Then throw in the tactical side of the race – the team play, the setting up of their top rider to have the best chance. And take into account all the micro competitions that go on in the wider event: the race to be the best mountain-climber, the best sprinter, the most aggressive rider, the best young cyclist. The whole thing is incredible.

And, of course, you take all of those elements and plonk them into some of the planet's most spectacular scenery, with a course running past vineyards and through medieval villages, over the Alps and the Pyrenees, through famous cities such as Paris, Nice and Bordeaux. Following this race on the ground is a must-do for any sports fan. You'll experience the best of France, while getting up-close to cycling's stars at their most important race.

Following this race on the ground is a must-do for any sports fan.

Sport: Golf
See it: UK

FAST FACTS

· The first Ryder Cup match was played in 1927, at the Worcester Country Club in Massachusetts, USA.

· Until 1971 the Ryder Cup was only played between the USA and the UK.

· US golfer Phil Mickelson holds the record for the most Ryder Cup appearances, with 12.

It's not often you get to cheer on a team, or even a country, in the sport of golf. Yes, you might have your favourite players, and they might hail from the same place you do, but they don't wear colours and they don't have cheer squads. They're just people, doing it for themselves. That is, until a certain biennial event rolls around. Until a group of American golfers dons the red, white and blue of their homeland, and a group of Europe's finest dons blue attire, and they take to the course for the Ryder Cup.

This has quickly become one of golf's most cherished tournaments, a chance for fans to see their favourite players take on the world – or take on the USA, as the case may be. The tournament shifts around, held alternately in the US and in Europe, though arguably the best venues are in the traditional home of golf, the UK, at courses such as Gleneagles and the Belfry. To watch this tournament on TV is one thing; to actually be there, seeing the world's best in action, to cheer for a team and celebrate a victory, is something else.

The best venues are in the traditional home of golf, the UK.

Sport: Tennis
See it: England

FAST FACTS

· More than
  34,000 kilograms
  (75,000 pounds)
  of strawberries are
  consumed by fans at
  each tournament.

· The COVID-19-related
  cancellation of the
  2020 Championships
  was the first since
  World War II.

· For garden nerds, the
  courts for Wimbledon
  are sown with
  perennial ryegrass.

Few tournaments are as historic, as iconic or as enjoyable as the Championships at the All England Lawn Tennis and Croquet Club – otherwise known as Wimbledon. Come for the tennis, stay for the strawberries and cream. Drink a Pimm's and lemonade in what is hopefully the sunshine. Sit on the hill and enjoy the party atmosphere while watching the big screen. Soak up all of the on-court drama, the wins and the losses, the joy and the tantrums, all conducted under the watchful eye of British nobility.

This tournament was first held in 1877, and sometimes it can feel as if little has changed since: the players are still separated into categories of 'ladies' and 'gentlemen', they still wear all-white outfits, they're still required to bow or curtsy to the Queen and the Prince of Wales, and they still play on grass, a surface rarely used throughout the rest of the world. The Championships also continues to be one of the most prestigious sporting titles on the planet, and an event that any sports fan would want to experience.

Soak up all of the on-court drama, the wins and the losses, the joy and the tantrums.

LEAP OF FAITH

Sport: BASE jumping
See it: Switzerland

You can imagine the pulse racing in the jumper's ears as they stand there on the cliff-top, considering the leap. There's a pause as they wait for the time to be right, for the wind to drop and the air to settle and to work up the nerve to make that final, irreversible move. And then they just do it. They flex their legs, they leap forward and they're gone.

This is BASE jumping in Switzerland, where the sport, somewhat curiously for a safety-conscious nation, is legal. The most popular spot to jump is around the small alpine town of Lauterbrunnen, which, via a few large gondolas, provides access to numerous high-quality BASE-jumping sites. Some 15,000 leaps of faith are estimated to be taken here each year.

Lauterbrunnen is popular not just with jumpers but with those who would like to witness the participants in action. Stand on the floor of the valley and you'll see parachutes opening up above you. Take a gondola up to Mürren or Grütschalp and you'll be able to sit by the take-off points and watch as daredevils pause, breathe … and then disappear.

FAST FACTS

· BASE stands for building, antenna, span and earth – the four categories of fixed objects to leap from.

· This is one of the most dangerous sports in the world, 43 times more dangerous than skydiving.

· Carl Boenish is considered the founder of modern BASE jumping. He died on a jump in Norway in 1984.

Sport: Paragliding
See it: France

FAST FACTS

· Paragliders are
  defined by having
  no rigid primary
  structure, unlike a
  hang-glider.

· The world distance
  record is a flight of
  588.27 kilometres
  (365 miles), held by
  Marcelo Prieto, Rafael
  Saladini and Rafael
  de Moraes Barros.

· The highest ever
  flight was 8157
  metres (26,761 feet),
  by Antoine Girard in
  Broad Peak, Pakistan.

There's a beautiful simplicity to the
sport of paragliding, with nothing but
a wing made of nylon or polyester to
send a participant soaring through the
sky, often covering amazing distances.
No engines, no solid structures, no
propellers. Just nylon, strings and
a harness.

Paragliding can be done in a purely recreational
way, enjoying the view and testing your skills as
a pilot, picking the updrafts and staying in the
air as long as you desire. This is also, however,
a competitive sport, with disciplines including
cross-country flying, aerobatics and endurance
races that combine hiking and flying. In France
there are more than 25,000 registered fliers and
the governing body for air sports, the Fédération
Aéronautique Internationale, was founded here.

For those keen to get in the air, there are schools
and joy-flight operators throughout France, though
the best sites are in the French Alps. Those
hoping to watch the experts in action should head
to Montclar, in the heart of the Alps, where the
annual Ubaye Paragliding Contest is held.

Asia

Sport: Naadam
See it: Mongolia

FAST FACTS

· Mongolian archers fire their arrows at targets from 75 metres (246 feet) away for men, 65 metres (213 feet) for women.

· Up to a thousand horses have been known to participate in the races at Naadam.

· Mongolian wrestling is untimed; wrestlers compete until one touches the ground with any body part but their hands or feet.

First, you need to know about the Three Manly Pursuits: wrestling, archery and horseriding. It doesn't take long in Mongolia to realise why these three sports are held in such high regard. This is a unique and traditional society of genuine nomads who still live in felt gers, hunt for food, travel on horseback and value physical strength. Of course wrestling, archery and horseriding would be revered.

For confirmation, simply attend Naadam, an annual festival dedicated to the Three Manly Pursuits in Ulaanbaatar. This is the most important cultural event on the Mongolian calendar, and it's a feast for the eyes, as arrows are fired, oiled-up men in leather underwear tackle each other to the ground, and children as young as five race wild horses over distances up to 30 kilometres (18 miles). You have never seen anything like Naadam before. It's exciting, it's bewildering, it's physical and it's culturally unique.

You have never
seen anything
like Naadam
before. It's
exciting, it's
bewildering,
it's physical and
it's culturally
unique.

·

Sport: Buzkashi
See it: Afghanistan

There's a point at which this game gets crazy, and you'll know when we get there. To begin, let's set the scene. You're in Afghanistan, or maybe Kyrgyzstan, or somewhere else in Central Asia. There are two teams, maybe ten on each side, maybe 12, though only four or five will be on the field at any one time. All players are on horseback. There's a field, about the length of two football fields, with goals at each end. The game is much like polo, only there are no mallets, and instead of a ball the players use a recently beheaded goat or calf carcass.

Right: there it is.

Buzkashi was invented by the nomadic Turkic people of Central Asia, and its popularity remains in the countries that now make up that region. Teams compete intensely – with whip usage allowed – to pick up the animal carcass and drop it into their goal at the other end of the field. It's a national obsession in Afghanistan in particular, where the best players are stars with sponsorship from the rich and famous. If you can't make it to Kabul for your next sporting holiday, however, buzkashi is also popular in Kyrgyzstan.

FAST FACTS

· Buzkashi is a Persian word, which literally means 'goat pulling'.

· The carcasses used for buzkashi are soaked in cold water for 24 hours to toughen them up.

· Though buzkashi competition is fierce, players can only whip their horses, not their opponents.

Sport: Sepak takraw
See it: Malaysia

FAST FACTS

· Sepak takraw is also played in Canada and the USA, thanks to South-East Asian migrants.

· The name is the Malay word for 'kick' and the Thai word for a woven rattan ball.

· The game is thought to have originated in Malaysia in the 1400s.

Wow. That's the word you will utter when you see your first game of sepak takraw. How do these guys get so high in the air? How do they twist themselves into those positions? How do they land without breaking something? Sepak takraw, a sport native to South-East Asia, is basically volleyball, only the ball is a small rattan sphere and players can't use their hands to control it. What that results in is both male and female players leaping high into the air and performing entire somersaults in order to 'spike' the ball using their feet over a high net into their opponents' court.

You will find this sport being played throughout Malaysia, Indonesia, Thailand and Laos, everywhere from dusty clearings in rural villages to modern stadiums with huge crowds. The most important competition is probably the Asian Games, which Thailand has tended to dominate. However, the best way to experience sepak takraw is at the humble amateur level, watching scratch matches played among locals where you'll witness seemingly normal people do amazing things.

GETTING A KICK

Sport: Martial arts
See it: Japan

So many of the world's most famous martial arts have their origins in Japan: karate, judo, jiu-jitsu, kendo, aikido, battō and more. These arts are forms of self-defence – they involve striking, wrestling, swordsmanship and the use of other weapons – but they're also training for the mind, with a strong focus on discipline, character, courtesy and respect. In other words, so much of what makes the Japanese mindset so fascinating as a whole can be seen in the country's martial arts.

If you visit Japan you will have limited opportunities to see martial arts in action, because competitions such as the Japan Martial Arts Championships are held only sporadically around the country. A much better way to gain an appreciation for the practice is to get in there and do it yourself. There are opportunities in all major cities to take introductory classes in swordsmanship, karate, jiu-jitsu, kyūdō (archery) and more.

FAST FACTS

· The famous crane kick from *The Karate Kid* isn't a real karate move – it was created for the film.

· The origin of Japanese martial arts dates back to training methods for samurai.

· There are two styles of Japanese martial arts: Koryu Bujutsu, or 'old school', and Gendai Budō, or 'modern'.

Sport: Sumo
See it: Japan

FACT FACTS

· There are six Grand
  Sumo tournaments
  each year, held in
  Tokyo, Osaka, Nagoya
  and Fukuoka.

· Sumo wrestlers
  aren't allowed to eat
  breakfast, but have
  a large lunch after
  training and then
  a nap.

· There are no
  weight divisions in
  sumo wrestling.

Taken on face value, sumo wrestling can seem a little simplistic. Two overfed guys get together in the middle of a circle and attempt to push each other out. Easy. And, on some basic level, Japan's most famous sport really can be that simple. But, of course, it's not. Not if you dig down into the traditions and the rituals. Not if you immerse yourself completely in this amazing sport and its cultural importance.

Spend some time in Japan attending tournaments and even witnessing training sessions and you begin to learn a little more about the nuance of sumo. The athletes embed themselves in the sumo world: they live together, eat together, train together, dress alike and even wear their hair alike. In the arena they follow a prescribed set of traditions linked to the Japanese Shinto religion: they stomp their feet, they toss salt on the ground, they perform movements to show they aren't carrying weapons. And then they try to push each other out of the ring.

Sport: Cricket
See it: India

FAST FACTS

- There are two women's cricket tournaments in India: the Women's One Day League and the InterState Twenty20.

- India's most important match-up in any form of cricket is with neighbouring rivals Pakistan.

- Indian cricket star Sachin Tendulkar has been awarded the Bharat Ratna, India's highest civilian award.

It's difficult to describe just how much the good people of India love the game of cricket. This isn't a sport, it's an obsession. It's a religion, probably India's third most important, though some would argue it takes first place. Walk through any open space – known as maidans – in cities such as Delhi, Mumbai and Kolkata and you will see people playing cricket, sometimes with nothing but piles of bricks for stumps and planks of wood for bats. The game crosses all boundaries of race and class. Everyone is into it.

To experience cricket in India you could simply watch one of those scratch matches on the maidans, or even join in — you'll probably be offered the chance. The other option is to get along to a stadium to see an international Test or an IPL Twenty20 game, and witness the mania with which Indians support their local team. Huge crowds pack the stands, yelling and cheering, screaming for their own players and at the opposition. The atmosphere is dense and loud and intimidating. And like nowhere else on Earth.

The game crosses all boundaries of race and class. Everyone is into it.

·

TOP OF THE TABLE

Sport: Table tennis
See it: China

Here's how table tennis works at the Olympics: a bunch of players turn up, they're sorted into doubles and singles, they play a long knockout tournament, they try their best, and China always wins. Seriously, China *always* wins. Table tennis was introduced at the 1988 Seoul Olympics, and since then, of a possible 32 gold medals across both men and women, China has won 28. Since 2008 they've won literally everything. The Chinese love table tennis and they're incredibly good at it. You can't argue with those numbers.

Table tennis became popular in communist China after Chairman Mao Zedong announced it as the new national sport in 1952, the thinking being that it was a cheap and enjoyable game that could be played by people of all ages and abilities. Table tennis has retained its attraction, and you only have to wander through a recreation area in Beijing, Shanghai or any city in China, really, to see locals engaged in intense battle. Alternatively, switch on your TV to catch televised national tournaments such as the biennial All China Table Tennis Championships.

FAST FACTS

· In 2016 Chinese star Ma Long won all possible world singles titles in the shortest ever space of time.

· Ping-pong (the original term for table tennis) was invented in England, in the late 1800s, as an after-dinner diversion.

· China's women have missed only one Olympic gold medal: the women's doubles in 1988, won by South Korea.

Sport: Jianzi
See it: Vietnam

FAST FACTS

· Jianzi has a history of more than 2000 years, and has been used by the Chinese military for relaxation.

· Competitive jianzi is played in both singles and doubles formats for both men and women.

· Seventeen countries are now members of the International Shuttlecock Federation.

If you have visited China and Vietnam, you have probably already seen the sport of jianzi. Wander around any city in these two countries in the early morning and you will find people gathered in pairs, booting what looks like a large badminton shuttlecock back and forth to each other. This is jianzi, a game that's popular with both rich and poor, with men and women, with young and old. You'll see fit youngsters throwing themselves about, you'll see retiree couples gently moving back and forth. Everyone loves jianzi.

The game is simple and largely non-competitive. You have a 'jianzi', a shuttlecock, which is weighted at one end and has real or plastic feathers at the other, and the aim is to get as many kicks in as possible without dropping it. Though a more competitive game involving two teams and a net exists, in its most basic form no one wins and no one loses. The idea is just to get a little exercise. Perhaps the most enjoyable place to see jianzi being played is around Hoàn Kiếm Lake in Hanoi, Vietnam. Get up at dawn, grab your jianzi and head lakeside to join hundreds of locals doing the same.

Sport: Bull wrestling
See it: Laos

FAST FACTS

· Bull wrestling is also popular in Bosnia, Croatia, Turkey, India and Oman.

· The Hmong people migrated originally from China, and now live in Laos, Vietnam, Thailand and Myanmar.

· Phonsavan is also home to the Plain of Jars archaeological site.

You think you know what's about to happen. Bulls are circling a big clearing. Crowds are gathering. There's talk of a fight in the air. You're not sure you want to see this. An animal is about to die for entertainment. But then … it doesn't. Because this is not the bull fighting you think you know. In Laos, it's not man versus beast. It's beast versus beast. Two bulls are herded into the centre of a field and then goaded into fighting each other. The angry bovines lock horns, stamp their feet and push as hard as they can until one turns and flees, usually through a gap created by crowd members diving out of the way.

In Laos this is a tradition of the Hmong minority group, many of whom live in the eastern town of Phonsavan. It's here you have your best chance of witnessing a local bull wrestling event. These competitions often coincide with Hmong festivals, particularly New Year, which occurs around November or December. Follow the crowds, and keep an eye out for charging bulls.

This is not the bull fighting you think you know. In Laos, it's not man versus beast. It's beast versus beast.

Sport: Muay Thai
See it: Thailand

FAST FACTS

· Muay Thai fighters begin bouts with cloth tied around their heads and arms, an old military custom.

· Fighters once wore rope across their knuckles, though this was outlawed in the 1930s.

· Muay Thai is known as the 'art of eight limbs', as each fighter has eight points with which to strike.

There are two things to concentrate on at a Muay Thai bout in Thailand, two activities, two complicated sets of rules and etiquette to witness and puzzle out. The first takes place in the ring, as two fighters go at it with skill and intensity. Muay Thai is fierce, a style of kickboxing in which opponents can strike each other with fists, elbows, knees and shins. The moves are complex, the intricacies difficult to appreciate at first. But the excitement and the passion are palpable.

That's in the ring. But outside it there's something equally interesting going on. Muay Thai fans love to gamble, and there are always bets being taken. The fascinating thing is the way those bets are placed, with a system of gestures used by seated fans to show bookies who they want to bet on, the odds they're accepting and how much they want to gamble. Figuring this one out is just as hard as understanding what's happening in the ring.

You'll be able to catch Muay Thai bouts across Thailand, though the most atmospheric venue is Rajadamnern Stadium in suburban Bangkok.

The moves are complex, the intricacies difficult to appreciate at first. But the excitement and the passion are palpable.

.

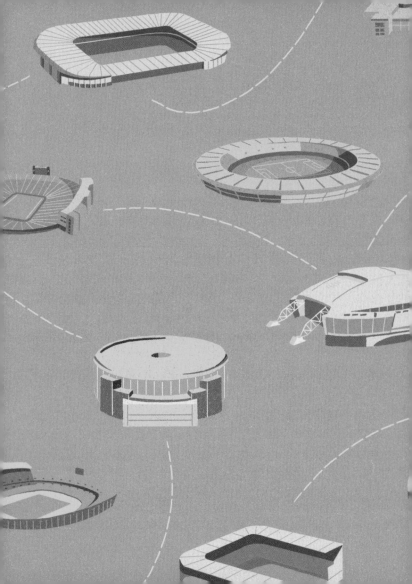

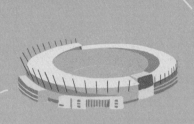

20 bucket-list stadiums

For sports fans, it isn't always about the game itself. Sometimes it's about the venue, a stadium or ground that could be as sacred and as cherished as anything that takes place there. For true sporting fanatics, a visit to these 20 venues over the course of a lifetime is a must.

.

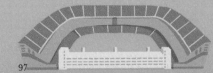

EDEN GARDENS

Kolkata, India

No touring cricket team looks forward to playing at Eden Gardens. For visitors, this 80,000-seat colossus of a stadium in sultry Kolkata is one of the hardest places in the world in which to compete, with its famously intimidating atmosphere, where proper riots have erupted on several occasions and where India rarely loses. For spectators, there's nowhere more memorable to watch cricket (see p. 88).

CAMP NOU

Barcelona, Spain

The home of Barcelona's famous football team is dizzying in size, with a capacity of almost 100,000, making it Europe's largest stadium. The atmosphere at any match here is electric, as some of the world's finest footballers take to the pitch in front of an inevitably full stadium of cheering, whistling supporters. To be here for a Clásico (see p. 61), a match against arch rivals Real Madrid, is to see sporting fandom at its finest. It's also worth taking a stadium tour.

FENWAY PARK

Boston, USA

Baseball is a sport that respects history and tradition, and no stadium has as much of either as Boston's Fenway Park. Built in 1912, the oldest in the Major League, the ground is as much a part of the Boston landscape as clam chowder and impenetrable accents. Fenway has plenty of quirks: attend a ballgame here and you'll become familiar with the 'Green Monster', the 'Triangle', 'Williamsburg' and 'Pesky's Pole'. You'll also become familiar with the people of Boston – and that has to be a good thing.

THE ALL ENGLAND CLUB

London, England

Mention 'SW19' to any sports fan and they will immediately know what you're talking about: Wimbledon. Home of the All England Lawn Tennis and Croquet Club, venue of the Championships, perhaps the most famous tennis tournament on the planet. Visit to indulge in some of the most English of sporting traditions, while seeing the world's finest players on court (*see* p. 76).

MICHIGAN STADIUM

Ann Arbor, USA

Consider this: Michigan Stadium, with a capacity of almost 110,000, is the largest stadium in the USA, and the third largest in the world – and it's built for college football. That's right: college students. Amateurs. And yet the yellow-clad fans pile in week after week to see the Wolverines, the University of Michigan team, take to the field. The atmosphere – before, during and after the game – is phenomenal.

MADISON SQUARE GARDEN

New York, USA

Name any superstar of an indoor sport and there's a good chance they've played at Madison Square Garden. Any basketball player, hockey player, boxer, wrestler or UFC fighter – they've competed here. And name any rock star – they've played here, too. This is one of those venues that truly deserves the title of 'iconic'. Try to get here at least once.

SAN SIRO

Milan, Italy

This imposing football stadium – capacity 76,000 – is the home of two of Europe's great football clubs, AC Milan and Internazionale, and when either of those teams plays there's sure to be a big crowd. However, when they play against each other, when all of Milan comes to a standstill and fans from each side pour in, there's nowhere else you would want to be. Stadium tours here are also excellent.

MURRAYFIELD

Edinburgh, Scotland

Pack your thickest clothes for a match at Murrayfield, Scotland's premier rugby venue, where the welcome is warm but the weather is not. It's worth braving the elements, however, at this 67,000-seater, which has been around since the 1920s and still attracts big crowds to see the Scottish rugby team in action. Murrayfield is a friendly venue where you're likely to leave with a slew of new companions, and possibly a cold.

ESTADIO AZTECA

Mexico City, Mexico

So much has taken place at Estadio Azteca. Diego Maradona's famous 'Hand of God' goal? It happened at the Azteca. His 'Goal of the Century': at the Azteca. The 'Game of the Century', between Italy and West Germany in 1970: at the Azteca. Not one but two World Cup finals: at the Azteca. This 90,000-seat stadium is one of football's great venues, and any match here will be memorable.

CROKE PARK

Dublin, Ireland

Ireland's premier venue for traditional games such as Gaelic football (*see* p. 66) and hurling (*see* p. 60) holds a special place in most locals' hearts. It's big, with more than 82,000 seats – the third largest in Europe – but it's also hugely atmospheric, a place to celebrate culture as much as to watch a sporting event, a traditional pilgrimage for fans from across the country.

MEIJI JINGU STADIUM

Tokyo, Japan

The USA has Fenway Park, and Japan has Meiji Jingu Stadium, a historic and much-loved baseball park that has been open since 1926 and retains so much of its past glory. This is the home of the Tokyo Yakult Swallows, a team with a passionate following of fans who twirl umbrellas and dance to J-pop every time their side scores a run. Babe Ruth played here once. Lou Gehrig, too. It's legendary.

LA BOMBONERA

Buenos Aires, Argentina

You think you've seen hardcore, passionate fans? Wait until you've seen Boca Juniors play at La Bombonera (*see* p. 28). The intensity of the support for the local team here is frightening, as flares are lit, drums are played, songs are sung, insults are yelled, and the whole stadium jumps and swirls like a single organism. The stadium is wedged into a narrow part of La Boca; the stands bear down on the tiny pitch in a similar way. Simply incredible.

AT&T STADIUM

Dallas, USA

Here's a part of the American sporting experience you don't want to miss: tailgating, when fans park their cars before a big game, set up barbecues and cooler boxes filled with drinks and party until it's time for kick-off. It's pretty much unique to the US, and it's at its best at AT&T Stadium, formerly known as Cowboys Stadium, a venue full of football- and barbecue-loving Texans.

BELL CENTRE

Montreal, Canada

The Montreal Canadiens take pride in their history: they're the only NHL team to have formed before the competition itself, and were part of the 'Original Six' clubs who founded the North American hockey league. These days the Canadiens are still hugely popular, and you have to get to the Bell Centre in downtown Montreal to appreciate just how seriously the locals take this game (*see* p. 10).

ESTÁDIO DO MARACANÃ

Rio de Janeiro, Brazil

Brazil's biggest sporting venue, with almost 79,000 seats, is unsurprisingly dedicated to the national obsession, football. It has also, unsurprisingly, played host to far more than 79,000 people. The record attendance here is a phenomenal 199,854, for a World Cup match in 1950. Even without crowds like that, this is one of the world's great venues, where Brazilians gather to celebrate their national passion.

ANFIELD

Liverpool, England

Almost every football fan has heard of 'the Kop', and even those with just a passing interest would recognise the strains of 'You'll Never Walk Alone'. Liverpool is an iconic football club with an iconic home base, Anfield. To be here at the beginning of a match, to watch as the fans in the Kop raise their scarves and sing their famous song as one, is to know just how important a club and a game really can be. If there's no game on, do a stadium tour.

MCG

Melbourne, Australia

If Melbourne is Australia's sporting capital, then the MCG is its parliament house, a huge venue used for cricket in the summer and AFL in the winter, a phenomenal stadium first opened in 1853, now with space for more than 100,000 fans. The annual AFL Grand Final is the biggest game of the year here (*see* p. 39); however, if you're in town around Christmas time, the Boxing Day cricket Test is also incredible.

LAMBEAU FIELD

Green Bay, USA

Lambeau Field, home of the Green Bay Packers NFL team, is something else. The vast stands here are populated by the 'Cheeseheads', the Packers' famously passionate fans, who even wear 'cheesehead' hats (the name is thanks to Wisconsin producing the most dairy products in the country). Lambeau is an open-air stadium where the weather gets bitterly cold (so cold the venue can even host ice hockey), but the fans' disposition is always warm. It's the oldest stadium in the NFL, packed with tradition, with a capacity of 81,441. It's a place you have to see.

WANDERERS STADIUM

Johannesburg, South Africa

When a stadium is nicknamed 'the Bullring', you get the feeling visiting teams don't exactly feel welcome, and that's very much the case at the Wanderers in Johannesburg. This is one of world cricket's most intimidating venues, where local fans take great pleasure in making visiting teams feel as uncomfortable as possible. It's well worth experiencing when the South African national team is playing. Its capacity? 34,000.

BORG EL ARAB STADIUM

Alexandria, Egypt

A lot of people know about ancient Egyptian culture, but what about the country's modern-day passions? To experience one of its most important, get along to see a football match at Alexandria's Borg El Arab Stadium, an 86,000-seater home to the Egyptian national football team, as well as local Smouha club. This is the Egypt no one ever tells you about.

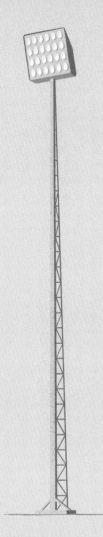

About the author

Ben Groundwater is an award-winning Australian travel writer and broadcaster who has been playing and watching sport since he could first walk. Ben has been a journalist for 20 years, beginning his career working on the sports desk at the *Sydney Morning Herald* before shifting his focus to travel. He's since become obsessed with sporting events and sporting culture around the world, attending everything from a Boca Juniors football match at La Bombonera to a stone-lifting tournament in a Basque Country plaza. His personal career highlight was winning 'Goalkeeper of the Tournament' at the Proserpine under-12s.

About the illustrator

In the UK you'll find the world's oldest football club, Sheffield F.C. This city is also home to the illustrator, Paul Reid. His work has featured in magazines and newspapers around the world, as well as across publishing and packaging projects. When he's not in the studio you can usually find him out walking with his dog. Or being used as a climbing frame by his two children.

Acknowledgements

Firstly, a huge thanks to the team at Hardie Grant Travel, whose support over multiple projects has meant so much. To Melissa Kayser and Megan Cuthbert in particular, I owe a huge debt of gratitude. I would also like to thank my tireless editor, Alexandra Payne, for her fantastic work on this book, and a big thanks to Megan Ellis and Michelle Mackintosh for typesetting and design.

On a more personal note, I would like to thank my partner, Jess, who has done the hard yards at home for the last few years, allowing me to travel and experience so much that went into this book while she does the often-thankless tasks of looking after our kids. Jess, I see you, and you are incredible. Thank you.

And lastly, a big thank you to my dad, Peter, for all of those afternoons in the backyard playing cricket, for all those Saturdays spent coaching my boyhood football teams, and for all those evenings sitting with my brother and me watching endless reruns of our video of England's Italia '90 World Cup campaign. This could never have happened without you.

Published in 2021 by Hardie Grant Travel,
a division of Hardie Grant Publishing

Hardie Grant Travel (Melbourne)
Wurundjeri Country
Building 1, 658 Church Street
Richmond, Victoria 3121

Hardie Grant Travel (Sydney)
Gadigal Country
Level 7, 45 Jones Street
Ultimo, NSW 2007

www.hardiegrant.com/au/travel

 A catalogue record for this
book is available from the
National Library of Australia

NATIONAL
LIBRARY
OF AUSTRALIA

Hardie Grant acknowledges the Traditional Owners of the country
on which we work, the Wurundjeri people of the Kulin nation and the
Gadigal people of the Eora nation, and recognises their continuing
connection to the land, waters and culture. We pay our respects to
their Elders past, present and emerging.

World of Sports
ISBN 9781741176919

10 9 8 7 6 5 4 3 2 1

Publisher
Melissa Kayser

Proofreader
Shawn Low

Typesetting
Megan Ellis

Project editor
Megan Cuthbert

Design
Michelle Mackintosh

Editor
Alexandra Payne

Cover designer
Josh Durham

Colour reproduction by Megan Ellis and Splitting Image Colour Studio
Printed and bound in China by LEO Paper Products LTD.